The Civil War

PRISON CAMPS OF
THE CIVIL WAR

Linda R. Wade

ABDO
Daughters Publishing

Visit us at
www.abdopub.com

Published by Abdo Publishing Company, 4940 Viking Drive, Edina, MN 55435.

Printed in the United States.

Graphic Design: John Hamilton
Contributing Editors: John Hamilton; Alan Gergen; Elizabeth Clouter-Gergen
Cover photos: John Hamilton; Digital Stock
Interior photos: David J. Eicher, pages 12, 15, 17, 19, 21, 24
              Digital Stock, pages 1, 5, 7, 22
              National Archives, pages 8, 9, 11, 14, 20, 25, 26, 27

Sources: *Historical Statistics of the United States to 1970.* U.S. Department of Commerce—Bureau of the Census; Jordan, Robert. *The Civil War.* Washington, D.C.: National Geographic Society, 1969; MacDonald, John. *Great Battles of the Civil War.* New York: Collier Books Macmillan Publishing Company; Miller, Trevelyan Francis, ed., *Prisons and Hospitals. The Photographic History of The Civil War in Ten Volumes.* New York: Castle Books, 1957; Morris, Jeffrey, and Morris, Richard. *Encyclopedia of American History (7th ed.).* New York: Harper, 1996; Robertson, James I., Jr. *Civil War! America Becomes One Nation.* New York: Knopf, 1992; Ward, Geoffrey. *The Civil War.* New York: Knopf, 1991.

Library of Congress Cataloging–in–Publication Data

Wade, Linda R.
    Prison camps of the Civil War / Linda Wade
        p. cm. — (The Civil War)
    Includes index.
    Summary: Looks at the situation of prisoners in the Civil War, where they were held, their care, and eventual exchange or release.
    ISBN   1-56239-822-9
    1. United States—History—Civil War, 1861-1865—Prisoners and prisons—Juvenile literature. [1. United States—History—Civil War, 1861-1865—Prisoners and prisons.] I. Title. II. Series: Wade, Linda R. Civil War.
E615.W27 1998
973.7' 71'—dc21   97-37479
                                                                CIP
                                                                AC

CONTENTS

INTRODUCTION

During the Civil War, being captured and imprisoned was a horror shared by soldiers of both the North and South. In all prisons, Union as well as Confederate, conditions were so bad that survival was considered a miracle. Great numbers of men suffered and died. Inadequate medical facilities and personnel caused many deaths. Then overcrowding, lack of food and shelter, contaminated water, disease, and untended war wounds added to the numbers. Just the rigors of weather and climate caused much misery. Death was everywhere.

Sometimes the deplorable conditions caused prisoners to go insane. There was little hope that conditions would improve. Both the North and the South were trying to win the war. The proper care of prisoners was far from a priority on either side. With neither time nor money for the care of enemy prisoners, prisons in both the North and the South were mismanaged. For many, prison became death. For those who survived, existence in the camps was a living death.

Facing page: Confederate prisoners under guard.

CHAPTER 1

PRISONERS OF WAR AND THEIR FATE

Because neither the Union nor the Confederacy expected the Civil War to last very long, no preparations were made for large numbers of prisoners of war. In fact, few officers were trained to operate prisoner-of-war camps. A great many men died needlessly as a result.

Both governments directed their main efforts toward winning the war. They improvised as they went along.

When it became apparent that a policy for prisoner handling was necessary, the governments of the North and South met. They set into motion the Dix-Hill Cartel. This paper set the terms of parole and exchange of prisoners.

Periodically, the two governments would officially exchange prisoners. The exchange was simply a "swapping" of prisoners on paper. It was made on a one-for-one basis, though higher-ranked officers had a higher value than soldiers of lower rank. The exchange kept the number of prisoners on each side relatively the same. Prisons were not necessary under such a system.

Under parole, a Civil War prisoner signed a promise not to take up arms again. In many instances, the parole was made on the battlefield. The prisoner simply went home.

Confederate prisoners captured at Gettysburg.

Parole and exchange also had monetary benefits. The conquering army did not have to provide for the prisoners' needs. The money saved could be used to finance the war.

Though the Dix-Hill Cartel was a good idea in theory, it did not work for long. Some soldiers let themselves be captured so that they could return home to rest or to plant or harvest their crops.

Keeping records of these numerous exchanges was difficult. Furthermore, many prisoners violated the parole.

There was another problem, too. It was the South's treatment of Northern black soldiers. The South regarded black soldiers as runaway slaves. They refused to treat them as legitimate prisoners of war. Confederate policy was to execute or enslave them. However, the South did not always carry out this order.

Lieutenant James B. Washington (left), a Confederate prisoner, with Captain George A. Custer of the Union's 5th Cavalry.

Finally, Secretary of War Edwin M. Stanton stopped the exchanges. If prisoners were taken, they would have to be placed in prisoner-of-war (POW) camps.

The earliest Confederate camps were near Richmond, Virginia. By 1863 there was a serious drain on Richmond's dwindling food supply. There was also the constant threat of attack. Prison security was hard to maintain.

Sometimes they used forts and civilian jails. Libby Prison was actually a large commercial building. They also used huts and tent camps. Andersonville in the South had an open stockade.

Around 150 military prisons sprang up between 1861 and 1865. They cared for more than 400,000 captive soldiers. Of these, 194,000 were Union soldiers and 214,000 were Confederates. Early in the war, the conditions in some of these places were tolerable. Later, the problems included overcrowding, poor sanitation, and inadequate water and fuel supplies. Added to this list were a poor diet and a lack of proper medical attention. These combined to make prison life miserable.

In all, some 30,000 Union soldiers died in Southern prisons. About 26,000 Confederates died in Northern prisons. The health of thousands more men was ruined for life. The record high for deaths during a single month of any prisoner-of-war camp was at Camp Douglas in Chicago, Illinois. Of the 3,884 Confederate prisoners held in February 1863, 387 men died.

Prison conditions, rather than willful mistreatment, caused most of the deaths. Poorly clothed Southern soldiers could not stand the harsh Northern winters. Northern soldiers suffered from the intense heat of Southern summers.

But the worst prison was the South's Camp Sumter in Georgia. It was simply known as Andersonville. Opened in February 1864, it was designed to hold between 8,000 and 10,000 prisoners. Plans to build barrack huts were abandoned because materials were not available.

General William Hoffman, commissary general of prisoners (at right) with his staff on the steps of his office in Washington, D.C.

Andersonville Prison, Georgia, held 52,300 Union prisoners during its one-year existence. Of those men, 13,200 died.

Prisoners had to make their own shelters from whatever they had. They used blankets, oilcloth, or just burrows in the ground. By August 1864, 33,000 men were confined within a 27-acre stockade. Part of this area was a swamp. Food, which was scarce in the Confederate army, was even scarcer for prisoners. Within 11 months, more than 12,000 Union soldiers died.

CHAPTER 2

ANDERSONVILLE

T he South needed prison sites far from the war. Andersonville, Georgia, was chosen. It was a small community of 20 residents in southwest Georgia. It had a railroad, a creek, and the climate was mild in the winter. The land was leased and officially named Camp Sumter because it was in Sumter County. Later, the prison would simply be called Andersonville.

Union captives at Andersonville Prison, Georgia, wait as rations are passed out.

🇺🇸

In January 1864, Confederate soldiers and slaves from nearby plantations began clearing the land. For six weeks, the sound of chopping axes, crashing trees, and thudding shovels echoed as the sandy soil was stripped of its lofty pines. The logs were cut into 20-foot lengths. They were hewed by hand so they would fit closely together. The timbers were then placed upright in a five-foot deep trench. They became the stockade fence around the prison pen.

The first 500 Union prisoners arrived at the Andersonville train depot on February 25, 1864, at 2:00 a.m. Cold rain fell as the men marched one-half mile (.8 km) to the prison site. Cold and wet, many could barely walk. When they arrived, they found no place to sit or lay down. Some stretched out in the mud and tried to sleep.

There was no shelter from the sun and rain. There were no bathrooms. Open trenches became bathrooms. The cookhouse had not even been completed. At first, rations consisted of corn meal, raw beef, and salt. The only pots and pans available were the ones brought in by the prisoners. It was very difficult to prepare what scarce food they had. The men soon realized they would have to take care of themselves by using what items they had with them.

Captain Richard B. Winder had overseen the building of the prison. His headquarters were in Andersonville because it was the largest camp. His presence there, however, did not make supplies any easier to obtain. The Confederacy was using all of its resources to fight the war and feed its own soldiers. Enemy prisoners were not an urgent concern. So the men used their blankets and overcoats to make little tents. They were called shebangs. Other men constructed huts and lean-tos. They used logs, tree limbs, bushes, shrubs, and brush that were left inside the prison by the construction crew.

Facing page: A section of the stockade at Andersonville.

 13

At the time the prisoners started arriving in Andersonville, only three prison walls had been completed. The fourth side was guarded by artillery. Sentry boxes, called pigeon roosts, were placed at intervals along the top of the stockade wall. Guards climbed ladders to the pigeon roosts and watched the prisoners.

Union prisoners began to arrive almost daily. As the number became larger, the rations became smaller. The wood supply dwindled to nothing. What food there was would be served on an irregular basis, some days not at all.

On March 25, 1864, Captain Henry Wirz arrived at Andersonville. He was now the officer in charge. He had been wounded early in the war and never fully recovered. He tended to be short-tempered. The ever-lingering pain of his wound, along with the difficulties connected with the prison did not help his moods. However hard he tried to operate the prison in an efficient manner, he was faced with ever-dwindling supplies. The number of prisoners grew so fast that he was never able to demonstrate positive leadership. His task was impossible.

Prisoners awaiting transfer at a railroad depot.

An example of the kinds of crude shelter available to the prisoners at Andersonville.

Soon after Captain Wirz took command, he ordered the building of a "deadline." This was a set of posts erected 15 feet (4.6 meters) inside the stockade wall. The deadline was put up to stop escapes by keeping prisoners away from the wall. Guards were ordered to shoot any prisoner who crossed over the deadline. The stockade fence had provided some shade. Now, even that little comfort was removed.

With the daily arrival of about 400 prisoners, space became an even greater problem. The men could barely lay down and stretch out.

Fresh water became another problem. The cookhouse was built above the stockade. The cooks tossed all their garbage in the water. Two dams had been planned so that drinking water would be available. The latrines (toilets), called sinks, were to be below the second dam. However, they were never built. Therefore, the water became dirty and undrinkable. The smell alone was enough to make men sick. Since the stockade wall was so tall, few breezes entered the prison yard to clear the putrid air. On windy days, neighbors two miles (3.2 km) away complained of the odor.

The prisoners kept coming. Disease spread fast. Smallpox, scurvy, dropsy, and diarrhea were only some of the medical problems. By April 25, three months after opening, 2,697 sick patients had been treated, and 718 had died.

The first hospital was located inside the prison. Few fresh bandages were available, so sick men were treated with dirty cloths. Gangrene was a real problem because of so much infection.

The food became worse. Ground cornhusks were mixed in with the corn meal. This mixture was coarse and caused severe diarrhea. Sometimes the men received beans or black-eyed peas and a few ounces of bacon. Occasionally, molasses and rice were available. But often the beans were full of insects, and the meat spoiled.

Several diaries were written during these months. Some of the men talked about their "pet lice." They pretended to be training the lice for a "vermin fair." A favorite game was "odd or even." Each one put his hand inside some part of his clothing and pulled out what he could get a hold of and say "odd" or "even." Then they would count their lice to see who won that round. This humor helped some of the men keep their sanity.

Conditions were anything but funny, though. The men were always dirty and had terrible body odor. Soap was in great demand and short supply. Some men gave up and threw themselves across the deadline so the guards would shoot and kill them.

Thieves added to the misery of Andersonville. A group called the Raiders viciously pounced on anyone who had anything they wanted. This group was finally caught by Captain Wirz, and a police force formed by the prisoners called the Regulators. Six were found guilty of murder and sentenced to hang. From then on, only petty thefts occurred.

Graves of the six "Raiders" executed at Andersonville.

Time passed slowly for the prisoners. The cold nights of winter gave way to hot days of summer. The humidity climbed with the temperatures. Flies pestered the men. Mosquitoes bit them. Worst of all, the sun burned their weak and tormented bodies. Even the shebangs offered little protection.

Deaths climbed, too. In June, there were 22,291 prisoners and 1,203 deaths. The July prisoner count climbed to 29,030 and 1,742 deaths. August 1864 was the worst month. There were 32,899 prisoners and 2,993 deaths. The largest number of deaths on any one day was 127, occurring on August 23. The total number of prisoners at Andersonville during its one-year existence was 52,300. Of those men, 13,200 died.

A miracle happened that month, too. During a sudden storm, a fresh water spring opened just inside the west deadline. Some men reported that a bolt of lightning had hit the spot. No one cared how it happened. All that mattered was that the men had good fresh water, pure and continuously flowing. The prisoners called the little fountain Providence Spring. They were certain that it was a gift of God's divine providence.

Facing page: Providence Spring as it appears today at Andersonville.

General William Sherman did not march to Andersonville when he went through Georgia. Instead, he set up headquarters in Savannah. Prisoners were shifted about. The North and South resumed prisoner exchanges in March 1865. Andersonville Prison ceased to exist when the war ended in April.

As prisoners returned home, newspapers reported the horrible conditions. Pressure was put on officials to punish the commandant. In May 1865, federal army officials arrived in Andersonville to arrest Captain Wirz. He was then taken to Washington, D.C.

A military court tried, convicted, and sentenced Wirz to hang. They said he had conspired with Confederate officials to "impair and injure the health and to destroy the lives. . . of large numbers of federal prisoners. . . at Andersonville." The sentence was carried out on November 10, 1865. His sentence is still debated today.

Meanwhile, President Lincoln knew it was important to identify the burial sites of dead prisoners. He contacted Clara Barton. Known as the Angel of the Battlefield, she had been a nurse in the Civil War army camps and on battlefields. Lincoln asked Barton to determine the location of missing Union soldiers and to notify their relatives. In August, shortly after arriving at Andersonville, Barton raised the United States flag in the center of the cemetery. Then work began by enclosing the cemetery and identifying the graves of the dead prisoners.

The execution in Washington, D.C., of Captain Henry Wirz, the Confederate officer in charge of Andersonville prison camp.

The graves of rows upon rows of Union prisoners at Andersonville.

She was helped a great deal by Private Dorence Atwater. He had secretly written the names and numbers of all the dead prisoners. He carried his list in the lining of his coat when he was exchanged in March. He then took the list to the War Department in Washington, D.C. He felt that the families of the Andersonville dead were entitled to know about their dead sons, husbands, and fathers. With his help, all but 460 of the graves were identified. These were inscribed simply with the words, "Unknown U.S. Soldier."

Andersonville was proclaimed a National Cemetery in November 1865. In 1970, Congress authorized the Andersonville National Historic Site to serve as a memorial not just to the men who died in Andersonville, but to all Americans who have ever been held as prisoners of war.

A visit to Andersonville Prison is an experience that is not soon forgotten.

CHAPTER 3

OTHER PRISONS

While Andersonville may have been the worst camp, men still suffered and died as a result of their imprisonment in over 150 other prisons. Libby Prison was one of the worst. Major Thomas P. Turner was the commandant of both Libby Prison and Belle Isle. Both of these prisons were Confederate and located in Richmond, Virginia.

Altogether, about 125,000 Northern soldiers were held in Libby Prison. Captured Union officers were often taken here. Libby Prison has been called a tobacco warehouse. Actually, it was a food

Libby Prison, a converted warehouse in Richmond, Virginia.

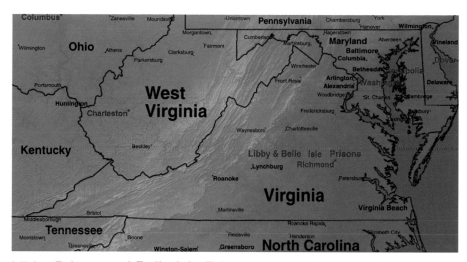

Libby Prison and Belle Isle Prison were both located in Richmond, Virginia.

warehouse. The name on the building read: "Libby and Sons, Ship-Chandlers and Grocers." Doors at the back of the building were on the James River, where ships could take on supplies. The building had three floors and a basement. There were eight rooms. When the military took over, all furniture was removed. Prisoners had to sleep on the bare wood.

In the beginning conditions were acceptable. Floors were washed and a makeshift bathroom was installed. However, as inmates poured into the building, conditions worsened. Lice, fleas, and flies constantly tormented the men. The conditions became so bad that it was compared with Andersonville.

Sleeping became difficult as the building filled with prisoners. The men found it necessary to sleep in shifts, lying on their sides close together. This not only saved space but also helped to keep them warm on the cold nights.

Escape was a constant dream. On February 9, 1864, 109 Union officers made an escape through a tunnel. Forty-eight were recaptured, 2 drowned, and 59 reached Union lines.

The ruins of Belle Isle Prison, near Richmond, Virginia.

Belle Isle Prison was located on an island in the James River, near Richmond. During the summer of 1863, life in the prison was acceptable. However, when the weather turned cold, life for the imprisoned men became extremely difficult. On November 18, 1863, 6,300 men were held captive. The camp had provisions for only 3,000. Tents were ordered, but never came. Many prisoners had to lie on the cold camp ground without any protection. On March 5, 1864, the medical inspector reported that one-fourth of the inmates were sick. The only thing done to help the men was to hurry the building of Andersonville Prison.

Another notorious prison was Camp Douglas. It was a Union prison located in Chicago, Illinois. Originally, it was a large instruction and recruiting camp. Then the prison was added.

Camp Douglas was built on low ground, and therefore it flooded with every rain. Mud became a constant problem. The barracks were poor, and conditions were unsanitary. As with all the other prisons, the more prisoners, the more unbearable life became for the men. In February 1863, out of 3,884 prisoners, 387 died.

Fort Johnson was a Union prison located near Sandusky Bay, Ohio. It was chosen as a prison site late in 1861. The prison was expected to be sufficient to accommodate all the prisoners taken during the war. This site, located on the west end of Lake Erie, was picked "in order to avoid too rigorous a climate." A prison fence enclosed 17 acres. Sentry posts were set up outside the fence to guard the two-story high barracks. After the first year, it became a place to send captured officers. It housed as many as 3,000 men.

At Aiken's Landing, Virginia, the steamer *New York* waits for an exchange of prisoners.

Even though this site was chosen because it seemed not to be so cold, the soldiers from the Deep South suffered from the severe winds that whipped across Lake Erie. Blankets were in short supply. Some of the men froze on New Year's Day in 1864.

Elmira Prison Camp housed thousands of Confederates in Elmira, New York. It was first chosen as a prison in May 1864. Prisoners began to arrive on July 6. The first shipment brought 649 men. During the month, 4,424 more came. In August, 5,195 men were brought to the camp. From September 1 to May 12, 1865, 2,503 were added. Conditions grew worse by the day.

The site of the prison had been badly chosen. It was below the level of the Chemung River. A lagoon of stagnant water caused much sickness. The winter weather added to the misery of the Southern

A baseball game between Union prisoners at Salisbury Prison, North Carolina.

Old Capital Prison, a Union prison in Washington, D.C.

soldiers. Many men became sick. One-fourth of the inmates died in the 12 months of its existence.

The same story is told over and over. Prisoners suffered a great deal in the various camps.

In all the prisons, boredom was a great problem. The men made up games. Some trained their pet "lice." They dreamed together and talked of their families. As some neared death, friends promised to get messages to their families. Occasionally, a new person would bring in fresh ideas to pass the time. But for the most part, time in prison was spent trying to survive.

CHAPTER 4

THE END OF MISERY

When at long last the war was over in April 1865, all the prisoners were released. They went home crippled. They went home hungry. Their strength was gone. For many, their health was gone. But they went home.

Home was a place many thought they would never see again. But open arms greeted crippled, hungry, and sick men. The open arms belonged to the women who had stayed behind helping in ways they had never helped before.

The courage of the people who lived during the Civil War is amazing. Regardless of the circumstances, they struggled on. They did what they had to do. They struggled to survive—to reach home.

INTERNET SITES

Civil War Forum
AOL keyword: Civil War

This comprehensive site on America Online is a great place to start learning more about the Civil War. The forum is divided into four main groups. In the "Mason-Dixon Line Chat Room" you can interact with fellow Civil War buffs. The "Civil War Information Center" is especially good for historians and reenactors, and includes help with tracking down your Civil War ancestors. The "Civil War Archive" is full of downloadable text and graphic files, including old photos from the National Archives. When you're ready for more in-depth information, the "Civil War Internet" group provides many links to other sites.

The United States Civil War Center
http://www.cwc.lsu.edu/civlink.htm

This is a very extensive index of Civil War information available on the Internet, including archives and special collections, biographies, famous battlefields, books and films, maps, newspapers, and just about everything you would want to find on the Civil War. The site currently has over 1,800 web links.

These sites are subject to change. Go to your favorite search engine and type in "Civil War" for more sites.

PASS IT ON

Civil War buffs: educate readers around the country by passing on interesting information you've learned about the Civil War. Maybe your family visited a famous Civil War battle site, or you've taken part in a reenactment. Who's your favorite historical figure from the Civil War? We want to hear from you!

To get posted on the ABDO & Daughters website, E-mail us at "History@abdopub.com"

Visit the ABDO & Daughters website at www.abdopub.com

GLOSSARY

Artillery

Weapons, especially cannons used in wars.

Commandant

The person in charge of a prison.

Confederate Army

Southern army.

Deadline

A set of posts that were set 18 feet inside the stockade walls at Andersonville. To go past the deadline meant instant death because guards were ordered to shoot to kill.

Dix-Hill Cartel

An agreement that set up the terms of parole and exchange of prisoners of war during the Civil War.

Fresh Water Spring

A fountain of fresh water coming from the ground.

Gangrene

Decay and death of skin tissue when the blood supply of a living person is interfered with because of injury.

Lice

A small biting or sucking insect that often attacks prisoners and causes much discomfort.

National Cemetery

A place of burial for men and women who served in the military. Many Civil War battlefields have a national cemetery where those who died in the battle are buried.

Parole

A conditional release of a prisoner.

Pigeon Roost

A small platform placed at a 30-yard interval along the top of the stockade walls at Andersonville. Guards sat and watched the prisoners, shooting any that tried to escape.

Prisoner

One held against his or her will by another individual or group, usually during wartime.

Regulators

Police force formed by the prisoners at Andersonville to help protect others against theft.

Runaway Slaves

Slaves who left their masters without permission. They usually went North seeking freedom, often using the Underground Railroad (a network of homes that protected and gave direction to slaves as they tried to escape those who searched for them).

Shebang

Little tents made from the blankets and overcoats of the incoming prisoners. Shebangs were the only protection from the weather.

Ship-Chandler

A dealer who supplies ships with necessary stores.

Stockade

A barrier of large, strong posts set upright in the ground.

Union Army

Northern army.

INDEX